W9-CPX-304

Make a Face

Allan Ahlberg

Colin McNaughton

Frog
Boy + Boy
Make a Face
Legs

RANDOM HOUSE NEW YORK

First American Edition, 1986.
Copyright © 1985 by Walker Books Ltd. All rights
reserved under International and Pan-American Copyright
Conventions. Published in the United States by Random
House, Inc., New York. Originally published in Great Britain by
Walker Books Ltd., London.

Library of Congress Cataloging in Publication Data: Ahlberg, Allan. Make a face. (Red nose
readers) Contents: Frog—Boy + boy—Make a face—Legs. SUMMARY: Labeled pictures
introduce vocabulary and concepts such as parts of a whole and adding. 1. Vocabulary—
Juvenile literature. [1. Vocabulary]
I. McNaughton, Colin. II. Title. III. Series: Ahlberg, Allan. Red nose readers.
PE1449.A348 1985 428.1 84-27744
ISBN: 0-394-87192-8 (trade); 0-394-97192-2 (lib. bdg.)

Manufactured in Singapore

1 2 3 4 5 6 7 8 9 0

Frog

a frog

 a big frog

a big
fat frog

a spotty big fat frog

a lumpy spotty
big fat frog...

…with a hat on

Boy + Boy

sun   +   sea

+ bucket   + shovel

+ shells   + sand

\+   ball   +   ice cream

\+   donkeys

= vacation

flower + water = big flower

pig + dinner = big pig

boy + boy + boy + boy

+ boy + boy + boy + boy

+ boy + boy + boy + boy

+ boy + boy + boy =

a pile of boys

Make a Face

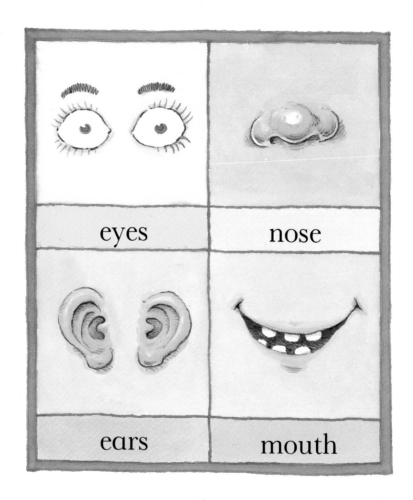

eyes · nose · ears · mouth

make a

face

fries

eggs

cake

apple

make a

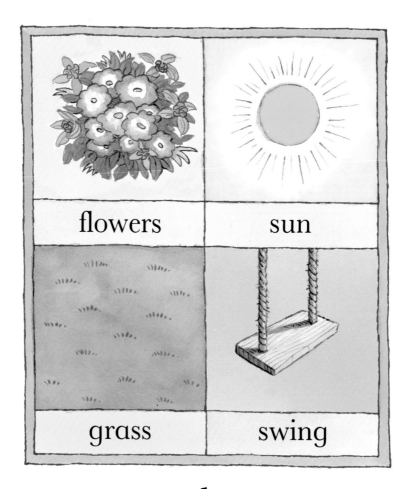

flowers

sun

grass

swing

make a

garden

toothbrush	teddy
slippers	stairs

make a

bedtime...

Legs

one leg

two legs

three legs

four legs

five legs

six legs

lift off!